MY CANCER
GOD'S MERCY

RAY SCOTT
Survivor Stage 4 Colon Cancer 1992

RAYMOND SCOTT

Library of Congress Cataloging-in-Publication Data is available.
ISBN 979-8-88738-577-8
ISBN 979-8-88738-578-5 (ebook)

COMPREHENSIVE
BLOOD & CANCER CENTER

Outsmarting Cancer

**Medical Oncology
& Hematology**
Ravi Patel, MD FACP
Alan D. Cartmell, MD FACP
Shawn C. Shambaugh, MD
David Kanamori, MD
Richard Ng, MD FACP
Pradip K. Rustagi, MD FACP
Wilbur Montana, DO
Rishi Patel, DO
Susana Bell, RN MSN NP PA-C
Kathy Jo Robb, NP-C
Kristi Mendez, NP-BC
Gurmit Singh, PA-C
Alan Thomas, PA-C

Radiation Oncology
Ajay Desai, MD
Giridhar Gorla, MD
Rodney Beaty, PA-C

Breast Surgical Oncology
Stuti Tambar, MD

Gynecologic Oncology
Jonathan Tammela, MD FACOG
Jeremy Cruz, NP CRNFA

**Skin Cancer, Dermatology
& Laser Center**
Neal Ammar, MD
Geover Fernandez, MD
Annaliese Prusse, PA-C
Darren Board, PA-C

**Otolaryngology (ENT),
Facial Plastic Surgery**
Sherif Ammar, MD

Infectious Disease
Randolph Senining, MD

Mind & Body Medicine
Naina Patel, MD

Naturopathic Medicine
Kalyan Gaddam, ND BHMS

(661) 322-2206 Main
(661) 322-7027 Fax

www.cbccusa.com

6501 Truxtun Avenue
Bakersfield, CA 93309

UCLA Jonsson Comprehensive
Cancer Center TRIO-US Site

July 19, 2020

Ray Scott is a truly remarkable man. I have had the privilege to be his oncologist for more than twenty-five years. In those decades, we have been doctor and patient struggling against a dread disease; more importantly, we have been friends and brothers in Christ. I have seen Ray at his highs and his lows. Regardless of his circumstances, he has always "walked by faith." Together we have walked through the valley of the shadow of death and emerged from the far end of that dark canyon into God's bright day.

In this memoir, Ray recounts his struggle with a medically incurable cancer through the lens of his steadfast faith in a loving Christ. Even as death was approaching from a medically incurable, relentlessly progressive cancer, Ray persevered in his faith. Through that same faith, he was directed to a faith healer and received an astonishing, medically impossible healing. He has remained in remission from his cancer throughout the subsequent decades. Following his miraculous healing from cancer he has continued his steadfast, faithful walk with Christ, a continual blessing to his family, friends and community.

As you read, you will be refreshed in your faith as you are drawn into Ray's story and see the power of the Lord at work. It is my hope that you will understand how this same love and power can be at work in you as well.

Alan Cartmell, MD, FACP

Bakersfield, California

With many thanks to my editor, Sheri McCarthy, with writewell.com and my webpage designer, Bob Hollis with Mobius Intelligent System, LCC – bob@mis.systems

TABLE OF CONTENTS

FAITH FOUNDATION

I was eight years old when I first learned about God's healing. Our priest, Father Grabowski, at St. Francis Cabrini Church in Piscataway, New Jersey was comforting our neighbor after her husband died. I listened with an open heart as Father Grabowski assured Mrs. Meyers that since her husband was with God in Heaven, he was completely whole and able like he had been in his youth: strong, healthy, and standing tall with God. There was something about the way he spoke to her that caught my mind. It was the first time I fully understood God's abiding love.

My family was faithful in our attendance at the local parish, and Father Grabowski was one of the first men outside of my family who shared things with me that became my inspirations in life. He was friendly and kind. He often talked to me about sports and music as we prepared for Mass when I was an altar boy. I enjoyed feeling the reverence for God the rituals of the Catholic Church upheld, and I continue to have deep respect for the traditions of the church.

Ours was a traditional home in the 1960's: my father and mother both worked. We ate dinner together every night, sitting around the dining room table in front of a meal cooked by my mother. A compliant child, I was one of the second sets of twins in my family. Growing up as one of six siblings, I knew I would never be alone. My three brothers and I all shared a single bedroom.

I was not shy, but I was quiet. I liked to sit silently with adults and listen to their conversations. I found it a joy to please adults around me, and, even as a young boy, I had a deep understanding that if I took care of others, God would take care of me. That deep sense made Cub Scouts, Boy Scouts, and community service natural fits for me.

My siblings and I attended Catholic school, and I learned to revere God by doing His will and to honor God by loving others as He loves me. The song of my heart was the prayer of Saint Francis: "Lord, make me an instrument of your peace." My favorite movies were "The Ten Commandments" and "Fiddler on the Roof." These movies gave me a sense of the importance of both God and family in my life.

My uncle George planted seeds of a deeper relationship with God. He was a godly inspiration who quietly spoke to me about a relationship with Jesus as something personal, not as a religion of man.

My desire to serve and be a part of things bigger than myself led me to join Cub Scouts, Boy Scouts, marching band, cross country, drama club, yearbook club and become a student leader of the first thank you Canada committee, a club created to thank Canada for rescuing our fellow Americans out of Iran in 1979. We created a petition that I was able to present to the Canadian Embassy in the World Trade Center in 1980.

After high school, I left New Jersey for California to run cross country at Taft College, becoming Taft's first long distance runner. I continued to serve others through student government, church choir, working with the college maintenance crew, coaching at nearby elementary schools, and teaching marching to the local junior high drill team.

My community efforts were acknowledged when I received the Taft Chamber of Commerce "Co-Citizen of the Year" award in 1982. While the Chamber had never given the award to two people before, the vote by three different groups resulted in a tie each time, so I shared the award with an adorable young lady named Carla Deann Uhles.

My faith led me to serve, and I did so without reservation, which was not surprising since I came from a strong faith family. My mother's family generously donated their own land for the Catholic Church to build a parish in Gardner, Massachusetts. The rectory was built right next door to my grandparents' home. I believe their active faith allowed for an extra measure of God's favor in my life. I did not know how much I would need His divine favor when I joined the United States Marine Corps in 1983.

MARINE CORPS

My decision to join the Marine Corps was met with concern by a few people in my life. My parents feared I was not aggressive enough to stand up for myself. They saw me as the son who had always been compliant and well-behaved. One of the leaders in our church, who was anti-military, told me she did not believe I was tough enough for the Marine Corps. When I made my final decision and told her I was enlisting, she ended our friendship.

My uncle Russell Scott, a Marine who served honorably in Vietnam, mentally prepared me for boot camp by explaining the severe physical treatment I could expect and how I should react to those challenges. He based his explanations on his own boot camp experience during the Vietnam era. Physically, he knew I was capable of excelling since I had been a college athlete, but he wanted me to be mentally prepared, not taken by surprise at the difficulty of the experience. Thankfully, the '80's version of boot camp was much less intense than his description of his own Vietnam-era experiences.

I joined Third Battalion, Platoon 3015, on November 18, 1983 and started boot camp at Parris Island near Beaufort, South Carolina. It was not quite a month after the bombing of the United States Marine Corps barracks in Beirut, Lebanon that killed 241 U.S. military personnel, making it the deadliest single-day death toll for the U.S. Marine Corps since the Battle of Iwo Jima in World War II. Our drill instructors would talk to us each night about tensions in the Middle East and say, "we are preparing for war, men."

I was appointed as first squad leader because of my college degree, which meant I was expected to help teach recruits to learn Marine Corps essential subjects. This comprised all the important information Marines are required to know during their service. I took on the task willingly and viewed it as a way I could serve my fellow Marines. Even in the Marines, I found a way to serve.

The base chaplain requested I be appointed as platoon lay leader after he noticed my regular attendance at weekly church services. This position meant I would lead recruits in prayer each night. I was recognized by my fellow recruits and my instructors as a spiritual leader, which eventually led to me being challenged for my faith.

One day, the junior drill instructor was using colorful language to "dog out" a recruit for not following orders. The base chaplain, a Navy lieutenant, walked in at that moment and said to the junior drill instructor, "This Bible is intended for recruits Scott, but I believe you need it more." He gave the Bible to the instructor.

That night during hygiene inspection, the senior drill instructor walked up to me, waved the Bible in my face, and asked if I could explain the reason for this. I immediately responded, "Request mast to a higher power," meaning request to speak with a higher authority in the military chain of command. The senior drill instructor was surprised by the immediate and correct response. He flipped the Bible at me and walked back to his office.

The incident did not end there. The next day was pugil sticks combat training which simulates fighting with one's rifle, normally one on one. The same junior drill instructor who received my Bible the day before had made other plans for me. He chose for me to fight two marines from other platoons, rather than just one. I stared at the two recruits and immediately prayed for some favor from God. A whistle would begin the fight. I heard it and attacked them knocking them both down before they could strike. There was only one problem. The whistle I had heard was for the match *behind* me. Thankfully, I was disqualified for my false start and saved from having to fight a huge Marine whom I witnessed doing serious physical harm to his opponents. Although I do not generally enjoy being disqualified from anything, in this case, I saw it as an example of God's favor protecting me from harm.

My high Armed Services Vocational Aptitude Battery (ASVAB) test scores meant I qualified for and was expected to go from enlisted boot camp to Officer Candidate School (OCS) with only with my battalion commander's approval, a common standard at the time. Just before graduation from boot camp, I met with the battalion commander to discuss this possibility.

Our conversation centered around my physical fitness test score. I scored 295 out of a possible 300. He wanted to know why I failed to score a perfect 300. I explained that my score was 295 because my hand slipped off the pull up bar due to sweat. I told him that my uncle, who was a warrant officer, prepared me for boot camp. Both enlisted and commissioned officers respect the rank of warrant officer. A warrant officer goes through the enlisted ranks to become a commissioned officer, proving both his physical and intellectual capabilities.

I went on to explain that I have always led by experience and not just by yelling orders out because of my rank. My statement apparently made him angry. The battalion commander said I needed more time in the Marine Corps to better understand my statement, which meant I would not be attending OCS. I replied simply, "Thank you, sir.

Just as I planned."

Since I was trained at Parris Island, near Beaufort, South Carolina, the common practice was to receive an order to be stationed at an East Coast base. However, God showed me favor again when I received orders for Camp Pendleton, near San Diego, California. The change made it easier to marry my adorable co-citizen of the year from Taft, Carla Deann Uhles.

When I first met Deann in college, her light brown hair, blue eyes, and kind smile warmed my heart, but I was dating her roommate at the time. We did not socialize, and when graduation time came, students were asked to vote between Deann and me for commencement speaker. This time, there was no tie. Deann gave a poised and heartening speech at our commencement.

Our first date consisted of a graduation party and a magical kiss under a streetlight. Not long after, she was hit by a car while riding the moped she used as her sole means of transportation. We had not been dating steadily, but I wanted to see her again before I left for an extended stay in New Jersey. We both felt a deep connection we could not explain. I told her I would return within a year.

Three hundred and sixty-four days later, I returned to Bakersfield and tracked her down through mutual friends. I called her and asked if she wanted to see me. She said yes, and I proposed to her just before I entered boot camp. We married after I was stationed at Camp Pendleton.

Deann and I shared a strong faith in God, though I was Catholic, and she was Baptist. My priest from Taft College, Monsignor Brown, performed his first interdenominational marriage when he conducted our ceremony at Our Lady of Perpetual Help in Bakersfield, California on August 24, 1984.

One day in the spring of 1984, a fellow Marine and I had a spirited discussion about our faith while we readied ourselves for weekend leave. We were surrounded by our squad, and we maintained our mutual respect as I argued the tenets of Catholicism and he argued the tenets of his Baptist faith. Whether it was that conversation or the years of respect I held for Deann, I was open to receiving more from God. Lying in my bunk that night, I asked God to completely fill me with his Holy Spirit and accept me for His will.

God's favor included divine protection evidenced throughout my time in the Marine Corps. I was sent to Egypt in 1985 to serve at Operation Bright Star. Operation Bright Star is a joint multi-lateral, multi-national military exercise held every two years in Egypt. It is usually a series of combined and joint training exercises led by the United States and Egyptian military forces.

Bright Star is designed to strengthen ties between the Egyptian Armed Forces and the United States Central Command as well as demonstrate and enhance the ability of the Americans to reinforce their allies in the Middle East in the event of war. These deployments are usually centered at the large Cairo West Air Base.

I was assigned to set up two field exchanges in Al Hammam, 275 miles from the Libyan border and 125 miles from the Cairo West Air Base. In this position, a fellow marine and I were to transport the exchange cargo supplies to Al Hammam, armed only with our wits. Together, we traveled across Egypt with no rifle, no interpreter, and with an Egyptian commercial driver who knew only two phrases in English: Coca Cola and Michael Jackson.

About halfway between Cairo and Al Hammam, we pulled up to a military check point, and the driver left the truck running while he got out to show his documentation. An Egyptian soldier opened the door to the truck and reached over to turn off the engine. My fellow marine and I tried to use hand gestures to stop him and explain that the truck would not start without being pulled and jump started. Startled, the Egyptian soldier pointed his AK47 rifle at me, and we immediately motioned for him to have his way with the ignition. He turned it off. We sat on the side of the road for an hour before the driver was able to flag down another truck to pull us along and get the motor running again.

After successfully setting up the two field exchanges in Al Hamman, I was assigned to run the field exchange for the Marine Corps air wing back at Cairo West Air Base. It was there that I learned a saying that would resonate deeply later in life: "No man is too big to pick up another man's foreign object or debris." The meaning of the saying was that it only takes a small piece of trash or bolt being sucked up into a jet engine to bring it down.

As the exchange officer for this location, I was required to bunk in the officer's tent next to the container with all the merchandise. It was out of the ordinary for a corporal to fraternize with officers, but since I was appointed to oversee the exchange, I fell into an exception.

I sold all the merchandise early and waited for my transport to take me to Cairo where I would meet up with fellow exchange marines to fly home. During the last days of the operation, I saw the general's helicopter fly onto the base. I jokingly said to one of the captains in the officer's tent, "Hey ask the general if I could catch a ride with him to Cairo." The statement was funny because it was ludicrous for a lowly corporal to request a lift from a general. He outranked me by twelve ranks.

I was casually strolling around in shorts, a t-shirt, and sandals on the other side of the compound when I heard my name broadcast over the speakers. "Corporal Scott, get back to the officer's tent now." I ran to the tent and saw three captains hurriedly packing my gear. When they saw me, they yelled for me to get dressed. The captain to whom I had made the joke to ask the general to give me lift said simply, "You got what you asked for."

The general's staff came to escort me out to meet the general, who said he would be glad to give me a lift. When his staff opened the helicopter doors, all I saw were colonels and lieutenant colonels. The good-humored general asked, "You men wouldn't mind holding the corporal's gear as we fly?" I was strapped in next to the machine gunners set on the outside of the helicopter.

As the wind whipped my face, I smiled inwardly. I could never have imagined I would be given the opportunity to fly with a general, while colonels and lieutenant colonels held my bags. Flying through Egypt, I looked down to see the great Nile River and the great Egyptian pyramids. My body moved in harmony with every turn of the helicopter, and I thanked God for His favor and protection during this operation. Spending a month in Egypt gave me a deeper level of gratitude for my country. I understand firsthand the statement, "One is blessed to live in America."

Upon the successful completion of my duties during Operation Bright Star, I was transferred to the USMC base in Barstow, California, where I was promoted to Barstow base exchange chief. I was assigned to a logistical support unit (LSU) that required a top-secret clearance, further combat training, and the requirement to obtain a Class A commercial driver's license.

During the interview process, while standing in front of the base's commanding general, I was asked because of my experience as a religious lay leader in boot camp if I could fulfill the duties of the unit's chaplain. I replied without hesitation, "Yes sir." To me, this honor was a continuance of God's favor in my life as a Marine.

We experienced two deaths during my time with the unit, during which I called upon the Lord to help me help the men in our unit. I was called upon to pray for the families and my fellow Marines, and I represented our unit at their funerals.

One of my favorite Marines in LSU was Staff Sergeant Santana, a very direct component leader who taught me 1) to achieve your next rank, you must act and work as if you already own it, and 2) in leadership, if you start strict and direct with keeping standards, people have respect for you. If you attempt to lead by being easy, people will use you and attempt to go around you. As a leader, it is your responsibility to understand human nature.

My Class A commercial driver's license provided me the opportunity to drive the church bus in Barstow for our church's children's ministry. Our oldest daughter, Lindsey, rode with me every Sunday to pick up children from the community and bring them to church, where we would join Deann and our younger daughter, Ashley. Lindsey was a kind and gregarious child, able to easily befriend new children, making them feel welcome as they rode the bus for the first time.

I continued to use my skills to the best of my ability to serve both God and my country. God proved that he had my back by showing me favor in adverse circumstances. I had been assigned an assistant for running the exchange. He tested positive on a drug test after returning from a weekend pass, which meant he was court martialed and could potentially be imprisoned and dishonorably discharged. Instead of honoring the Marine Corps values of honor, courage, and commitment, he falsely accused me of stealing money from our exchange change machines to try to create some leverage he could use to seek a reduced sentence for his misconduct.

The staff judge advocate charged the military police (MP) with investigating. The MP chose to conduct very little research and instead simply charged me with a crime. I was called into the battalion commanding officer's office to talk about office hours for my military punishment for this unproven "crime." Instead of accepting the penalty for something I did not do, which would tarnish my reputation as a man of God, I rejected the office hours and requested a formal court martial. I called my pastor and asked for prayer. I needed wisdom to handle these false allegations. God had already placed me in the best position possible by making me a part of the LSU special operations unit. I would be answerable only to the base commanding general. Had I not been in special operations, I would have had to answer to the lower ranked unit commander.

I contacted the LSU commanding officer and explained the false allegations and pending charges. Within twenty-four hours, all charges against me were dismissed, and the investigators discovered that the only fingerprints found on the change machines were my assistant's. God had people move on my behalf when all I could do was pray.

The staff judge advocate of the Marine Corps made me a witness for the prosecution of my assistant in the court martial trial. The defense counsel commented about my faith during my deposition prior to the trial. During the court martial, the defense attempted to discredit my testimony in front of the military judge because of my faith by saying I was a "religious fanatic." The judge immediately stopped them. I simply answered, "I am a Christian." My assistant was found guilty, served time in military prison, and was dishonorably discharged from the Marine Corps.

God's favor during my Marine Corps service reinforced the role of faith in my life. I experienced even higher-level security and leadership during my time at Barstow. It was my experience in the Marine Corps that gave me complete understanding that the more apparent God's character was in my life, the more I could trust God to place others in my life to provide His protection and favor. I lived the Marine Corps motto: "Semper Fidelis" (always faithful).

I served in the Marine Corps until November of 1987. At the end of my enlistment, I met with the commanding officer for all Marine Corps exchanges from USMC headquarters in Quantico, Virginia. He gave me a great compliment upon ending my tour of duty. "Sergeant Scott," he said, "because of your business skills you have been assigned to the exchange service, because of your leadership skills, you belong in the infantry." I was among the first to receive the Navy Achievement Medal for my actions in the Logistical Support Unit.

God used the Marine Corps to strengthen my Christian character as well as my business and leadership skills. I never forgot a prayer from basic training that my senior drill instructor Staff Sergeant Graham prayed over our entire platoon. *"What is your life worth if you are not willing to lay it down for another?"* I could not know it then, but God used the Marine Corps to prepare me for the toughest battle of my life.

Presort
First Class Mail
ComBasePrice

U.S. POSTAGE >> PITNEY BOWES

ZIP 20373 $ 000.43⁹
02 4W
0000343914 OCT 20 2020

MR. RAYMOND P. SCOTT
BOARD PRESIDENT, KEEP CALIFORNIA BEAUTIFUL
8665 S. UNION AVENUE
BAKERSFIELD, CA 93307

29 September 2020

Dear Mr. Scott,

    Thank you for sharing your inspiring EBook with me and for the effort you put into creating this encouraging resource. This will make a great addition to our library at the Home of the Commandants.

    Many thanks for your thoughtfulness and for your dedicated service to our Corps and country. On behalf of all Marines, I wish you continued good health and all the best.

Semper Fidelis,

David H. Berger
General, U.S. Marine Corps
Commandant of the Marine Corps

Mr. Raymond P. Scott
  Board President, Keep California Beautiful
    8665 S. Union Avenue
      Bakersfield, CA 93307

BULLDOG FAITH AND THE HAND OF GOD

THE DEVIL WHISPERED IN MY EAR, "YOU'RE NOT STRONG ENOUGH TO WITHSTAND THE STORM."

TODAY I WHISPERED IN THE DEVIL'S EAR, "I AM THE STORM."

Deann and I settled in Bakersfield, California after I completed my service with the Marine Corps. Bakersfield is in the San Joaquin Valley and is important to both agriculture and energy production in California. It is also the birthplace of the country music genre known as "the Bakersfield sound." Our family began attending Kern Christian Center, led by a fellow Marine named Billy

Rash. The brotherhood of the Marine Corp was built on knowing a fellow Marine would always have your back and he would never leave you behind. He understood me, and I understood him. He has a sensible, straightforward personality and I related to his conservative, traditional mindset.

I found a job as an insurance salesman, and we rented a small, two-bedroom apartment from some friends of Deann. I continued to drive the red pickup truck I bought while I was in the Marine Corps, and Deann drove an Oldsmobile Cutlass. We did not have much materially, but we had each other, which was everything to me. We lived on my $22,000 annual salary, while Deann stayed home with the girls. Times were tough, but our hope for a happy life endured.

I became heavily involved with Kern Christian Center, serving as an usher, working with the men's ministry, and singing in the choir. KCC gave me the first opportunity to help with the construction of a new building, which I enjoyed. I also became involved in prison ministry through a pastor named Howie Steinhart, whose ministry was focused on the California Youth Authority prison system. Pastor Steinhart himself had been incarcerated numerous times, but had turned his life around and now worked tirelessly to bring hope to inmates with the news of God's love and compassion. I enjoyed Pastor Steinhart's authentic and direct manner as we traveled to various prisons. Once, during a five-hour drive to Preston Youth

Correctional Facility near Sacramento, we listened to David Wilkerson's "Bull Dog Faith" sermon. The phrase stuck with me because one of the main points was to hang on to God's Word as a bulldog would hang on to a piece of meat.

The bulldog mentality showed up in a dream in which I fought for my life with Satan himself. It felt like a true physical fight, similar to the hand-to-hand combat I had learned in the Marine Corps. Satan and I would punch, kick, and throw each other around the room in an effort to kill each other. A pivotal point in the dream was when Satan and I had each other by the throat. Satan laughed, trying to intimidate me. But, instead of cowering to fear and allowing him to win, I remembered that Satan wanted my heart and soul to destroy me and my faith. I mustered all the power I had within me, held tight to my faith, and punched Satan in his chest, my hand bursting through his body. I ripped out his heart, dropped it to the ground, and stomped on it. I released my hold and watched Satan crumble to the ground.

When I chose to go back into management and end my time in insurance sales, I continued living out my faith in my work as a manager of Olive Garden, the American casual dining restaurant chain specializing in Italian-American cuisine. I loved my job and the ability it gave me to serve others. I especially liked to work Sundays, as I got to see a lot of my church friends throughout the day.

Sunday June 7, 1992 started out like any other workday.

But when I pulled the door open, I felt some pain radiating across the right side of my abdomen. Throughout my lunch shift, the pain intensified, and, according to my employees, my face took on a yellow hue. This was different than the stomach pain and high fever I had experienced two weeks prior, which I had believed was food poisoning. It had literally been the worst I had ever felt. I even uncharacteristically stayed home from work the following day. I was like my father: I had a high pain tolerance and the ability to shake off the flu by going to bed and sweating it out. I had thought nothing of it until now when the stomach pain returned with a vengeance.

My fellow manager suggested I go home before I made anyone else sick, and I reluctantly agreed. He also suggested that, since I was in such bad shape, I should call my wife to come pick me up, but I knew Deann was busy with our girls, who, at nine and six, were happy and active, so I drove myself the ten miles home. Once I got there, it was evident to Deann that something was seriously wrong.

She was folding laundry when I walked in and collapsed on our bed. I began thrashing and kicking the bed in pain. Concerned, she asked whether I wanted to go to the urgent care center or the emergency room. Through gritted teeth and covered in sweat, I eeked out "emergency room." Deann flew into action. She found someone to care for our girls, and she drove me to Mercy Truxtun Hospital's emergency department.

The triage nurse told me my conflicting symptoms made me a nightmare to diagnose. When doctors discovered a hard bulge in the right side of my abdomen, they believed my appendix was ready to burst. I was rushed into surgery with a surgeon I knew, Dr. Stone.

Dr. Stone had repaired an inguinal hernia some months prior and, during that surgery, discovered I suffered from a severe reaction to anesthesia called malignant hyperthermia (MH). MH presents as muscle rigidity, high fever, and a fast heart rate. Complications can include muscle breakdown and high blood potassium. I am like most others with MR: normal when not exposed to anesthesia.

My propensity to negatively react to general anesthesia led Dr. Stone to choose a spinal block for my emergency appendectomy, which does not trigger MH. While a spinal block only lasts for about forty-five minutes, a simple appendectomy could be done easily within that time frame. Unfortunately for me, the appendectomy was not simple.

Once inside, Dr. Stone found that my appendix had long since ruptured. What I had thought was food poisoning two weeks prior was actually my appendix rupturing. He cleared away the sea of gangrene in my abdomen and found a fist-sized tumor among the inflamed membranes surrounding my inner abdominal wall. He removed the tumor and, in doing so, had to remove the critical ileocecal valve, which separates the small and large intestines, to gain safe margins around the tumor's location. He finished his work in ninety minutes. By the grace of God, the spinal block lasted the duration.

When I woke up in the recovery room, uncomfortable due to the drainage tube coming out of my nose, I was told I had a large mass removed. I called my mom in New Jersey, and I told her the doctor said they had removed a mass and that I was okay. Normally talkative, she was quiet with me on the phone that day. A nurse who was at the time the head of nursing development and training at Jersey Shore Hospital, she knew instinctively that it was cancerous.

The day after my surgery, Deann and I were watching Michael Landon in *Highway to Heaven* on the hospital television. It was the episode in which a pregnant mother was diagnosed with cancer. Dr. Stone walked in and broke the news that the mass was a large, stage four colon cancer. He wanted to know how I was able to walk around for two weeks with the amount of gangrene and peritonitis that had formed inside me. I did not have to pause to consider God's favor in my life once again. I simply responded, "That's God for ya."

Dr. Stone said I would walk out of the hospital, but because of the uniqueness of my cancer, which typically appears in people over age sixty, the hospital had called a tumor board of specialists to discuss my case.

Our family was absorbing the news of my diagnosis, but there was not time for it to settle in before we learned more devastating news. Deann's grandfather was diagnosed with bone cancer the same day I was diagnosed with colon cancer. It felt like being held at gunpoint by a double barrel shot gun. Our girls, Lindsey and Ashley, stayed with Deann's brother, Phil, during my hospital stay and had not been able to see me for few days. Lindsey, a mature and perceptive nine-year-old, noticed everyone's somber mood and asked, "Is everyone upset because my daddy died?" Our family assured her I was alive, told her what was happening in basic terms, and brought our daughters to me.

Once understanding what we were dealing with, I called my mom and told her what the surgeon explained. My mom had a new assistant working with her from Cedars-Sinai Medical Center in New York. She knew her assistant had oncology experience, so she said, "Tell me about a thirty-year-old male with stage four colon cancer." Her assistant replied, "Not good at all."

CALL TO PRAYER

prayer
pour out our hearts to God

Deann called Pastor Rash to come pray with us in the hospital. As soon as we finished praying, Dr. Stone arrived and began to explain that my cancer was extremely aggressive and that I may have only a maximum of eighteen months to live. Treatment would begin immediately. Radiation treatment five days per week for five weeks and a round of chemotherapy started a month after I left the hospital, allowing time for the surgery site to heal. The hospital sent a counselor to talk with me the very next day. She asked if I was mad at God about the cancer. I said "No, because I know that this was not from God, but from Satan." She smiled and then started asking about my family.

On the first Sunday after being released from the hospital, Pastor Rash asked if I would share my story. I planned on singing the song "People Need the Lord" after giving my testimony of God's provision during my stage four colon cancer diagnosis. I had not yet given my testimony when Pastor Rash called me up to sing during the time he was ministering to the congregation. It was out of the order I was expecting, which took me by surprise, but I began to sing. The Holy Spirit moved, and people began to come to the base of the stage as if it was an altar call. By the time I finished, twenty-five people were on their knees, worshiping God. I walked back to my seat and peace settled over me as I felt God speak "this is what this is for" to my heart. Philippians 4:7 (ESV), which reads "And the peace of God, which surpasses all understanding, will guard your hearts and your minds in Christ Jesus," became real to me in that moment. It gave me strength and allowed me to trust God with my life.

I began the radiation regime with no ill side effects, at least none that I could see. The thirty-minute treatments five days per week did not burn my skin, but I did not fully realize just how vulnerable my immune system had become until midway through the five weeks of radiation treatment. My daughter, Ashley, got the flu in July of 1992, and I picked her up to comfort her, as most fathers would. Later that night, I developed flu symptoms. Normally a miserable experience, my radiated abdomen meant the pain was incredible.

Deann helped me throughout the night, caring for me as she would another child. Finally, in the wee hours of the morning, I remembered the relaxing power of a hot bath. I climbed in and told Deann to get some sleep. The hot water worked: the pain lessened, and my abdomen loosened. I relaxed and let the hot water do its work. The house was quiet. Our girls were asleep in their bedroom next to the bathroom, and Deann was asleep in our bed. I sensed that I was going to make it through this battle and go on to fight the physical war my body was raging.

As dawn began to break, I stood up to get out of the bathtub and everything went black. The combination of my weakened state and the relaxing bath had drained my strength, and I passed out. My head hit the corner of our vanity and slammed into the wall. The noise woke my girls, who came running to find their dad lying naked on the floor, blood streaming from my head. They woke up Deann, and she wrestled me into our bedroom and onto our bed. My nine-year-old, Lindsey, sat on the end of the bed, taking in the gravity of the moment and said plainly, "This sucks." My six-year-old, Ashley, held my hand and comforted me with her childlike faith, "Daddy it's going to be okay." My heart ached with the weight of what I was putting my wife and daughters through. I had no idea how bad my battle would become and how tightly I would cling to the peace of God.

THE FIGHT OF MY LIFE

Chemotherapy began in August of 1992. I spent ninety minutes once per week at the oncology unit, listening to Phantom of the Opera as the drugs we hoped would save my life entered my bloodstream. The music relaxed me and gave me the opportunity to think about my girls: Deann, Lindsey, and Ashley.

Again, I felt God's favor in how few side effects I experienced. Deann found clumps of hair on my pillow each morning, but I never went entirely bald. Steroids kept nausea at bay, and instead of losing my appetite as I had been warned would happen, I had the opposite reaction. My appetite throughout chemotherapy *increased*. Though my energy was diminished, I was able to keep my job and work throughout 1992. My oncologist said my physical fitness going in helped me tremendously. All that time spent on the track and training in the Marines was paying off.

A blockage in my intestine required a second abdominal surgery in February of 1993. I was only able to take in fluids and instant oatmeal for three weeks, and doctors found the cancer had grown back at the original site. This required the doctors to remove 40 percent of my large intestine and 20 percent of my small intestine, resulting in a condition known as "short bowel syndrome." SBS created an inability to get enough nutrients and water from the food I ate, as well as the embarrassing consequence of incontinence. It was devastating to me to be unable to control my bodily functions. I was in a miserable state and did not smile or laugh for at least two weeks, which was contrary to my God-given personality. Deann was especially concerned for her Marine.

Finally, one late night, *Tim Allen: ReWires America* came on HBO and on my television screen. I had always enjoyed his humor and outlook on life. I found it relatable and authentic. My burden lifted for the first time in two weeks when his comedy show helped me shift my focus away from myself and onto other, less life-threatening things. Laughter, for me, truly is the best medicine.

Deann and I decided we wanted to change oncologists and met with Dr. Alan Cartmell of Comprehensive Blood and Cancer Center. We found him to be open to my direct questions and willing to answer me in kind. My initial question was, "After reviewing my case, what is your best educated guess?" Dr. Cartmell said he estimated I had less time than the eighteen months the tumor board had given me. I told Dr. Cartmell I was not going to let something the size of my fist take me out. Dr. Cartmell fired back in a surprised tone, "Ray, you must realize a tumor the size of your fist is not small!"

My surgeons, Drs. Stone and Newborough, found that the tumor had ruptured, spraying cancer cells throughout my abdomen. In layman's terms, it had the same effect as if a can of spray paint had been used to coat my insides. Only, the "paint," in this case, was cancer cells. Dr. Cartmell told me they would now have to surgically go in and look for the cancer every six months.

As I healed from the surgery that removed portions of my intestines, another physical storm was brewing. I noticed a sort of pressure in my abdomen, until I could eventually see something under my skin. As it turned out, what I had seen and felt was my intestine pushing through the abdominal wall—a hernia that had developed from my previous surgery.

Dr. Newborough operated to repair the hernia in October of 1993. Once again, a spinal block was chosen for this "simple" procedure because of my propensity for MH with general anesthesia. But instead of just a simple hernia repair, Dr Newborough found more cancer, this time growing on my back muscles.

The spinal block meant I was awake during the entire surgery, so I heard him say "Oh, *no*." This is not exactly what you want to hear when your body is cut open and your doctor is in the middle of an operation. I watched the nurse walk away with what he had just cut out of me to prepare it for further pathology testing. Dr. Newbrough began to physically examine each of my organs by touch, checking for any growths. The pressure was intense, and I had developed the type of relationship with my doctors in which I felt comfortable enough to say anything. I said, "Doc, just rip out my throat while you're up there." The sound of my voice surprised Dr. Newbrough, who looked over the apron and said, "What the heck?"

I spent an additional three days in the hospital riding a roller coaster of high temperatures and problems breathing due to a possible collapsed lung. My prayer changed from asking God for healing to asking for "God's perfect will." This change in my prayer life once again brought Philippians 4:7 (ESV) to mind. "And the peace of God, which surpasses all understanding, will guard your hearts and your minds in Christ Jesus." I held tightly to that promise.

Deann and our girls continued to have a difficult time with the effects of the cancer on our lives. In 1993, the American Cancer Society was able to help our girls cope through free private sessions with a therapist. That service was invaluable. I have always been appreciative of people who cared for the ones I love most: Deann, Lindsey, and Ashley. I have a deep love for the American Cancer Society because of the way they cared for my girls.

God used ordinary people who came in and out of our lives to bless us and bring peace. We were blessed by amazing people at Mercy Hospital who loved Deann and me, learned our names, and were generous with their kindness every time I was there. A hospital housekeeper named Maria who worked on the third floor cancer ward was a sweet, amazing person who loved on Deann and me with a peaceful and loving smile and prayer. Pete in radiology always made me feel special and took what seemed like extra effort to make me comfortable in my pain. The nurses of the third floor knew I was the general manager of Olive Garden and would talk to me about their teenagers and work issues. And they assigned roommates in need of encouragement to my room because they knew I would give it. I have a deep appreciation for nurses because of all I witnessed from my mother's work as a nurse. Therefore, since I could not eat most of the time, I asked my Olive Garden staff to bring meals to the nursing staff instead of to me, to show appreciation.

My battle intensified when, in February of 1994, it became clear that my cancer was not responding to the once-per-week chemotherapy protocol. Dr. Cartmell changed the chemotherapy protocol to a twenty-four-hours-per-day intravenous drip. While this change was vital in my fight, it also meant I had to give up my love of working and, instead, apply for federal disability. It was a devastating blow.

I developed an unusual pain in my neck during Easter weekend of 1994. At first, I tried to block it out of my mind so we could focus on the impending birth of our nephew and enjoy quality time with our family. But the pain had other plans. By the time I contacted Dr. Cartmell,

I was unable to turn my neck at all. He feared the cancer may have spread to my base of my neck and ordered immediate tests. The results of my liver test showed possible damage due to chemo, so I underwent a liver biopsy to determine the extent of the damage. At the same time, a failed port-a-cath caused a blood clot that, in turn, resulted in swelling my hand, arm, shoulder, and neck to three times their normal size. I needed blood thinners to resolve the clot, but because of the liver biopsy, doctors had to walk a fine line in administering the medication so I did not bleed out. I was in critical condition, and Deann and I were told I would probably not make it through the weekend.

My parents rushed from New Jersey to California to say their goodbyes. My mother, a nurse all her adult life, walked into my room, took one look at me, and immediately collapsed across my hospital bed sobbing, knowing this may be the last time she would see me. However, I made it through the weekend. And through the next week. I was heavily sedated on morphine, Lortab (acetaminophen and hydrocodone), and Valium, but I pushed on.

I woke up one morning with my fighting spirit fully in tact, and I decided I would get up and use the restroom on my own. I stood, fell in what seemed like slow motion, and took out everything in my path on my way down to the floor. It took four people to get me back into my bed, and I was instructed in no uncertain terms not to try that move again.

My situation was still precarious, but I promised Deann I would take her on a cruise for our tenth anniversary, more than six months away. My parents were with us in the room as I spoke, and since Deann's birthday also coincided with my parent's wedding anniversary, I went on to suggest we should all go together on the cruise. Of course, they agreed to my plan, so long as it meant I would be here in six months' time. It gave us all hope.

The cruise both occupied my mind and provided me with something to do while I was home on disability after being released from the hospital. I used our tax return for the deposit. It was an act of faith for me, but as the months went on and our prescription drug costs increased, I felt I needed to request a refund for such an extravagant expense. I had talked a lot about our upcoming cruise, and my oncology nurses always smiled in encouragement. One of my nurses, Rosaling, at Comprehensive Blood and Cancer Center, knew of my plans and also of my financial difficulties. She had lost her husband to colon cancer some time before and had also gone on a cruise with him before he died. She took a special interest in Deann and me and one day quietly asked if I would allow her to pay for our cruise. I felt the love of God through her gift. Now, I just needed to live long enough to fulfill my promise to Deann.

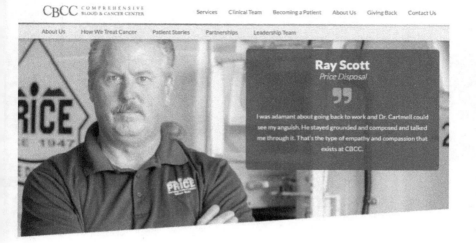

CBCC COMPREHENSIVE BLOOD & CANCER CENTER

Services   Clinical Team   Becoming a Patient   About Us   Giving Back   Contact Us

About Us   How We Treat Cancer   Patient Stories   Partnerships   Leadership Team

Ray Scott
Price Disposal

> I was adamant about going back to work and Dr. Cartmell could see my anguish. He stayed grounded and composed and talked me through it. That's the type of empathy and compassion that exists at CBCC.

What Ray Scott initially thought was appendicitis, turned out to be stage four colon cancer. At the young age of 30, he was faced with tumor complications so severe that it had engulfed his appendix.

Ray's health issues were so intense at the time that outside doctors were confusing and overshooting timelines for his life expectancy.

That's why Ray was appreciative with the open dialogue he had with Dr. Cartmell at CBCC. "He was so straightforward. I told him that I had 1.5 years to live... he told me this is not a small tumor Ray, we need to act fast."

Fighting Through Treatment

Ray's treatment course was extensive as his situation required surgeries, radiation, and chemo. Still, he went through it all with little to no obstacles.

"I was adamant about going back to work and Dr. Cartmell could see my anguish. He stayed grounded and composed and talked me through it. That's the type of empathy and compassion that exists at CBCC."

Coming Back to Life

Mr. Scott attributes his revival to God and to the CBCC physicians. "It's super important to have the right doctor. I should have died nearly four times, but together we took care of it."

He has been with us beyond his recovery, for 25 years, paying it back by volunteering at events such as 'Campout Against Cancer', and 'Relay for Life.'

Additionally, Ray has launched an e-book about his cancer journey, and is in the process of finishing another one. You can learn more from him in the link here: https://ordinarymanextraordinarygod.com

Cancer:
Colon Cancer

Diagnosed:
1992

Treating Physician:
Alan Cartmell, MD, FACP

This article was published in the *Bakersfield Californian* on Sunday June 7, 2020. This was the twenty-eighth anniversary of when I was diagnosed with my stage four colon cancer.

KEEPING MY PROMISE

Faith is trusting God even when you don't understand His plan

I caught a glimpse of myself in the mirror one day while preparing to take a shower. Where a bullet-proof Marine once stood, I saw a 130-pound dying man. I asked God to give me the same power He gave to the mighty men of Israel to defeat their enemy. I flexed what muscles I had left, like the World Wrestling Federation wrestlers I enjoyed watching. I continued this routine daily to exercise my faith and gain the strength to make it through another day.

In June of 1994, a new radioactive isotope test called an OncoScint was developed to detect cancer cells at a microscopic level. I took the test and it showed cancer growing at the base of my aorta. When the radiologist saw it, told Deann, "You know, Ray is terminal."

Dr. Cartmell delivered the formal results to us and said, "I know you want to go back to work, but that is impossible." My face flushed with anger, and I stiffened. If I had been holding a two by four board in that moment, I would have snapped it like a twig. Deann saw how upset I was and had to leave the room to compose herself. The emotional pain of hearing those words made me want to strike out at something. I did not yell or lash out, but the anger was so palpable that it scared my doctor. I took a deep breath and once again centered myself. I refused to allow myself to self-destruct. I reflected on my girls, and I centered myself with the thought that I had to continue to fight and be here for them. I took another deep breath and said, "What's next?"

My only option was to go into my fourth round of increasing chemotherapy. I was placed on a regime of drugs calculated for 125 percent of my body weight. The increase of drugs in my system caused mental difficulties that prohibited me from driving or paying bills. I simply could not focus for the length of time needed to accomplish those ordinary tasks safely.

I woke up from a nap on the couch after church in August of 1994 to find my chest wet. I realized immediately that something was wrong with the chemo pump. I called Dr. Cartmell's office, and a staff member instructed me to turn off the chemo pump, wash my chest with water, and come into the office the next morning. Every part of my skin that the medication had overflowed onto and touched turned black and began to peel.

A few weeks later, I tried to stain the backyard fence for my brother-in-law, Phil, to thank him for his generosity in keeping our car insurance paid while I was off work. I loved to work. I love to be outdoors, and since I was not allowed to work at my job, this was something I thought I could handle. However, when I stood up from a squatting position, I became dizzy and clung to the fence for support. Phil saw me unsteadily holding his fence, desperately trying not to pass out, and rushed me to my doctor's office. Dr. Cartmell discovered my body had rejected the port-a-cath and another massive blood clot had formed. I was immediately sent to Truxtun Radiology for an ultrasound to determine the severity of the blood clot they suspected.

You know it is bad when the doctor performing the test asks with forced nonchalance, "How are you feeling right now?" The blood clot was cutting off my left jugular vein, not allowing blood to pass. The doctor sent me straight to the emergency room at Mercy Hospital Truxtun, and they sent me up to the third floor, which was used for cancer patients. My mother and my sister, Kim, had already planned to fly out and spend their vacation time with me, Deann, our girls. We hadn't expected this fourteen-day hospital stay, but it was good to have them at our home to help with our girls.

While Mom spent her days with me, we talked about her father who had died well before my birth while she was in nursing school. I told my Mom I had always sensed that her father was a man of great size; I was surprised when she said he was not. Then, I said, "He must have been man of great stature." She was deeply moved. My grandfather was a great man of the community who helped build several homes in Gardner, Massachusetts, which is why they named a road after him. Mom told me about a conversation she had with a counselor at a Catholic church. She told the counselor about my situation with cancer, and the counselor asked her if she had asked her father in heaven to watch over me. I felt a great sense of peace from that.

In January of 1994, Deann and I were encouraged to attend Christ Cathedral, since the congregation had an amazing love for God. We were so physically and mentally tired from the roughest year of our lives. Senior Pastor Clyde Wasdin ensured us that the church would be a constant source of prayer and support for me, Deann, and our girls through the church's family groups, Koinonia. We began regularly attending there, and the influence that decision made on our lives is another form of God's favor.

Since I was scheduled to give my testimony at Christ Cathedral, I decided to practice my favorite song from my hospital bed. I lay with my eyes closed, headphones on, and cassette player on my lap. Eventually, I became aware of someone in my room. I opened my eyes to see four nurses smiling through tears, listening to me sing, "People Need the Lord." The night I gave my testimony and sang, Deann and I chose to trust God's perfect will for my life. If that meant me being another bass in His heavenly choir, we would accept that as the sovereignty of God in our lives.

I finished up my fourth round of chemotherapy in early October of 1994, and I felt strong enough to give back to the church that had done so much for my family, Christ Cathedral. I enjoy physical work, and I had no obligations taking my time, so I helped set up the annual fun fair, an event that served the surrounding community. The blessing of being with everyone encouraged me for what was coming next.

I had the second radioactive isotope test in October, and it showed the cancer continued to grow at the base of my aorta. On October 31, 1994, Dr. Cartmell entered the exam room, results in hand. He began, "Ray, we cannot talk about remission or recovery, only about the quality of life left, which is very short." Without hesitation, I said, "You, too, can be wrong." Dr. Cartmell once again smiled at me with amazement at my determination to live regardless of what the results said. He told me later that he, a fellow Christian who prayed with me each time we met, had to stop, take a moment, and breathe before entering the room because of my deteriorating condition.

The following week, we were scheduled to go on the cruise with my parents. Three days prior to our departure, I was admitted to the hospital for what we believed was an ulcer caused by the chemotherapy. Rosaling, who made our cruise possible, heard I had been admitted and came to the hospital to see me. Standing next to Deann, she jokingly said if I did not get out of the hospital, she was taking my place on the cruise.

I was released from the hospital the day before our cruise. My mom and Deann had already made the cruise line aware of my condition. They inquired about the cruise line's ability to handle medical emergencies and went so far as to ask about the capacity to have me air lifted off the ship if needed. I was not in good shape, but I was going to keep my promise to my wife.

My plans were to update my parents during our time together and relay the most recent test results and Dr. Cartmell's grim prognosis. I wanted to explain what we wanted for Deann and the girls if things progressed. My parents could then talk to my five siblings in New Jersey after the cruise to prepare them for what looked to be my end.

Deann and I picked up my parents at the Los Angeles International Airport, and from the moment we picked them up to the moment we dropped them off four days later, it was like God froze time and space. I had no pain whatsoever. We did absolutely everything I wanted to do aboard that ship without hesitation. As soon as Deann and I dropped my parents off at LAX, the pain immediately came back in full force. I was preparing for my end.

THE MIRACLE

"A Mother's Prayer"

Throughout my battle with cancer, both my mother and mother-in-law had their prayer groups praying for my healing. Rhonda, a woman in my mother-in-law's prayer group at Christ Cathedral, was a brand-new Christian who was just learning to listen to the voice of God. He placed in her heart to get me to the Benny Hinn Healing Crusade that would take place on November 17, 1994 in Sacramento at the Arco Arena. Rhonda made the effort to call the ministry and asked if I could enter through the handicap entrance due to my condition. Together with another woman from the prayer group, my mother-in-law and Rhonda made all of the arrangements for the motel and crusade.

Whenever I had to go on a business trip, I would always ask each of my daughters what they wanted me to bring them home. Deann took the lead for this trip and asked our girls separately, "What do you want us to bring you home?" Both of them answered the same way: "My daddy healed."

Benny Hinn is an Israeli televangelist, best known for his regular "Miracle Crusades"—revival meetings or faith healing summits that are usually held in stadiums in major cities. These are later broadcasted worldwide on his television program, This is Your Day. I knew of Pastor Benny Hinn from watching the Trinity Broadcasting Network for years prior to ever being diagnosed with cancer. I believed God could heal me when I asked for His perfect will.

The drive from Bakersfield to Sacramento takes five hours. I was in pain throughout the trip, and my abdominal discomfort signaled to me that I would need to look for a hospital soon. When I mentioned something about the pain, my mother-in-law said the pain was due to all the cancer cells running around saying goodbye to each other because their time was over.

We made it to the motel lobby to wait for the shuttle to

the arena. I leaned on a pillar in the lobby and looked at Deann, "Tell the ladies they need to pray because my legs are about to give out." I clung to that pillar and prayed for strength until our van arrived. We got into the van and made our way to the arena. We drove by the line to get in, which curled around the building, even though we arrived five hours before the start of the service. Thank God we were able to go through the handicap entrance, which was open and empty. We settled into our seats at the back of the arena on the first level. As I looked around, I recognized some of the ministry staff members from other crusades on television I had seen. They were overburdened with people asking them to pray for them. Being an usher myself, I asked the closest usher to pray for me in the middle of the arena floor.

I went back to my seat at the end of the row, near the restroom. I strategically chose to sit there, because I knew I would need to use the restroom frequently, and I did not want to disturb people by making them get up for me. I have always had a heart for single mothers, and I call Deann a "baby magnet." Sure enough, God placed an eighteen-year-old mother with a five-week-old baby girl in front of us. She sat together with her own mother, expecting God to move. The baby had Down syndrome and two holes in her heart, and this beautiful young mother had enough faith to bring her little girl for a healing.

Midway through the service, the "Hallelujah Chorus" was playing with nearly twenty-thousand people singing in one accord to usher in the presence of God. The little baby slept on her grandmother's shoulder; her hands stretched out toward me. I gently touched her hand and prayed, "God, take my life isntead of this baby's. For what is my life worth if I'm not willing to lay it down for another?" At that moment, I felt the power of the Holy Spirit go through my right side, where the cancer had started, to my right arm and hand to the baby's hand. I slowly released her hand and thanked God for this moment.

The split second I released the baby's hand, the same usher who had prayed for me five hours earlier tapped me on the shoulder. Stunned, I asked, "How did you find me?" He asked how I was feeling; it took me a moment to register his question because I was so engrossed in the baby. I quickly explained that all my pain was gone, and I had been going back and forth to the restroom all evening due to my condition, short bowel syndrome.

He must have been an usher captain or a ministry staff member, because he took my hand and walked me down the stairs to the floor of the arena, past all those standing in line to profess that God had touched them tonight. I checked in with the doctors who spoke with each person before going on the platform with Pastor Benny Hinn.

Deann and I went to the crusade hoping to receive strength to go through a fifth round of chemotherapy. I did not even imagine I would be called onto the stage. I was the third person on the platform that night. I stood in front of Pastor Benny, and he asked me to explain what had happened. I explained that a tumor had exploded in my abdomen, and I had been in pain all day. He placed one hand on my back and, with his other, began pushing on my abdomen, repeatedly asking me "Does this hurt?" When I answered, "*No*," he took two steps back and said, "In the presence of God, your cancer is dead." Deann and I both felt the power of the Holy Spirit fall upon us, and we were escorted off stage to give more details about what we believed God had done.

PROVING GOD'S WORK

The morning after the crusade, I called Dr. Cartmell's office and left him a message, saying "I am healed, and I want you to run the tests again." We returned home to our daughters with the gift of answered prayer. Dr. Cartmell was very cautious until we ran the blood work at CBCC lab. In yet another instance of God's favor, our medical insurance company authorized an expensive radioactive test normally only covered every six months. My previous test had only been six weeks prior, but there were enough physical changes in the results to constitute a repeat.

Four days after my healing, Dr. Cartmell ran the blood work, and when he saw the results, began laughing, astonished at the transformation from the previous blood work that had showed a man dying of malnutrition. Now, the results were that of a healthy man. Dr. Cartmell said it was super blood.

Dr. Cartmell said, "You have one of two options to choose from: believe that God healed you and live, or begin chemo round five with the treatment that we had planned for you." By now I'm sure you know the choice I made: to believe and live.

Strength and soundness immediately returned to me. The Saturday following the crusade, I was at an ambassador training for Promise Keepers. As I liked to do, I showed up early to give a hand to the crew setting up. The California state representative of Promise Keepers, who was doing the training, was a two-time All-American and NFL defensive player of the year, Randy Gradishar of the Denver Broncos. The former NFL linebacker towered over me, but he had a warm smile, and he welcomed me by asking what God had been doing in my life lately. I explained how God had just healed me a week earlier from a stage four colon cancer while I prayed for a five-week-old baby at a Benny Hinn crusade in Sacramento. His mouth dropped open, and he praised God for His power in my life. It felt like another show of God's favor to be able to share my testimony of God's healing power with a person of that status in such a simple conversation.

The following month, Christ Cathedral was planning on installing heavy wooden pews in their sanctuary to replace the chairs they had been using. The pews had been in storage for several years and needed to be moved, placed, and attached to the sanctuary floor. An installer from a pew manufacturing company would arrive four days before Christmas, work through the holiday, and complete the job the day after Christmas. I volunteered to run the crews to prepare the sanctuary and pews for installation.

I called on a dear friend, Dean Barthelmes, and his two sons to help me move the pews into the sanctuary. Pastor Wasdin was amazed yet scared as he watched me bench press pews that weighed over 200 pounds, move them into place, and lower them slowly over studs hammered into the floor to secure them.

I worked with the men of Teen Challenge to clean, space, and position the pews to be ready for the installer when he arrived. This would save time during the installation process and, in turn, save the church money. Because of our efforts, the installer was able to go home before Christmas. The energy I had to complete the pew project was more than enough proof for me that I was completely healed.

I demanded that Dr. Cartmell release me back to work. Dr. Cartmell said that normally a patient who had received this much chemotherapy would be kept on full-time disability for six months to recover. By the grace of God, and a little bit of a stubborn streak, I was back to work without restriction on January 2, 1995.

THE SECOND HALF OF THE MIRACLE

A man that hath friends mush show himself friendly:
and there is a friend that sticketh closer
than a brother.
Proverbs 18:24

Throughout my ordeal, I came close to death four times. It was God's people who encouraged me, from moment to moment, until I was at the right time and place for God to perform His miracle in my life. In the twenty-six years since the miracle, I have come to appreciate the friendships that supported me and my family on an even deeper level.

I am known as a serious individual, and I take friendship seriously. Friendships created with trust and loyalty through the difficult times in one's life make celebrating the good times more personal. God provided me with great friends before, during, and after the cancer journey that were of great support for me and my family, and he brought me several exceptional friends to enhance God's

67

will in my life since the cancer diagnosis. This is what I like to call, "the second half of the miracle."

One of my first calls after Dr. Cartmell released me to go back to work was to Della Equipilag, my area supervisor for Olive Garden. We had met in 1992 when we were fellow general managers. Della and I had similar work ethics, and she was promoted to area supervisor. I could not have been more fortunate to be under her oversight during the worst of the cancer. She has been a true friend who, through her direct nature, enabled me to improve and succeed. Her leadership during my experience made me realize that, in the corporate world, the people we report to have the greatest effect on our lives.

Della was thrilled to get the phone call from me that I was released to come back to work on January 2, 1995. I told her I would take on whatever she needed. Della did not hesitate to accept my offer to work with her again, and I became her kitchen manager. She used my talents for troubleshooting to help her with several Los Angeles restaurants. Della continued to share her insight and experience with me, which made me an all-around better manager. She taught me how to explain and walk people through my thought processes when sharing my vision and expectations with them. I've found this skill to be vital for successful management.

In 1997, Della left to work for Dick Clark American Bandstand Grill, a great family restaurant and dance club located in Columbus, Ohio, and Dick Clark's personal project. We continue to share insight for each other's careers and make time to visit with each other.

Another call went out to my dear friend, whom I call my "church mother," Lynn Neufield. Lynn, a nurse and fellow choir member at Kern Christian Center, had been inspired by God to help us pay for the medication I needed to help me through chemotherapy in 1992. Just like my mother, Lynn was a great resource for discussing medical issues, and the fact that she lived in Bakersfield was a bonus.

When I asked Lynn why she chose to love me, she said, "I feel God places certain people in our lives, and He did that with you. I knew you were a man of God after His own heart. I knew you needed help at that time in your life, and it so blessed me to be used by God. I instantly felt a closeness with you, like I had another son. What God has done in your life is amazing to me." Lynn put it best when she wrote the following:

> Being a brother and sister in the Lord was easy. I soon became Mom and Ray was son. Ray loved being a husband to Deann and father to two beautiful girls. It was easy to see he was content, especially in his love of his Lord and Savior.
>
> When Ray was diagnosed with cancer it was devastating news. Prayers went up and treatment started. It was very hard time for him and his family, but he never lost hope.
>
> When Ray first started treatment, God used me to help with expensive medications, and I was blessed to be a part of God's plans for Ray. Our God is a God of miracles, and he was healed.
>
> God has a mighty plan for Ray's life, and he, to this day, is doing God's will. Ray has been a blessing in my life, as he has for many others. Ray's obedience to God and doing God's will is Ray's testimony and a light to whoever meets him. I am proud and blessed to be Ray's church mom, and part of his life, and part of God's plan. A true healing. Amen!

Another steadfast friend of mine who loved me and my family through the hardest trial of our lives was Jim Fontana. We met while we both worked for a McDonald's restaurant in Bakersfield in 1989. A fellow serviceman from the Air Force, I knew God orchestrated our introduction because of the way we gelled together as a team. Jim helped me grow as a manager and as a person. He taught me things like keeping an organizational monthly task list to ensure operational success. It was so obvious we worked exceedingly well together that the area supervisor gave Jim and me the toughest stores to operate and expected a turnaround from the area supervisor and unit manager.

Troubleshooting required understanding how to

handle people and issues successfully. Because of our respect for each other's work ethics, becoming close friends outside of work was natural. We both appreciated time off watching World Wrestling Federation events and eating pizza with our wives and my girls. Jim became "godfather" to our girls in a true Italian sense. Even though life eventually took Jim to Phoenix, Arizona, my friend made trips back to Bakersfield in 1993 during the cancer treatments to check on me.

One day, during an eight-hour chemotherapy session, I woke up to find Jim quietly sitting next to me. He waited patiently until I realized he was there. Jim frequently reached out to Deann to discuss my progress and check on her and our girls. For me, a true friend does not have to have all the right words. Their presence is what is needed. Jim gifted us with his presence throughout my cancer journey.

Jim and I talk freely about faith, family, and friends with ease, because we trust each other. It doesn't matter where in the country we are, if there is an opportunity to be there for each other, we are. One summer, I was visiting my family in New Jersey while Jim was in a New Jersey hospital visiting his mother. Jim had just finished his degree at Arizona State University and wanted to share his accomplishment with his mom. I took the day to be with them at the hospital. Years later, when our daughter, Ashley, went to college in Phoenix, Arizona, Godfather Jim was there, and he assured me and Ashley that he would be there to care for her if she needed him.

Throughout our careers, we have shared our insights with each other, because we have known they come from a pure of heart. When Jim's dad died, I drove to Phoenix just to be there for him amidst all the emotions of the weekend. He did not need my words. He needed my presence. He needed me to listen, and he needed to know that I cared. This sharing of our lives has continued for more than thirty years now.

In the years since my healing, I have continued to enjoy the friendships God has placed in my life, especially the ones who have shown such love to Deann. Jeanette Herring is one of those friends. We met way back in 1988, and she was a rock for Deann when I was diagnosed. She became a rock for me, too, throughout my cancer treatment. Jeanette came to my hospital room at times when we were told I would not make it through the week. One evening, when I was heavily medicated, Jeanette said I gave a "sermon message" about my love for and marriage to Deann. Even in my delirium, I think my spirit knew she was an extra special friend to my wife.

After my miracle, Jeanette became the executive director for Bakersfield Centennial Celebration. She was responsible for seventy-two events over a two-year period, including raising funds for the creation of Bakersfield Centennial Plaza in the heart of downtown Bakersfield. Jeanette relied on my food management experience to help her with events, and, due to our common faith, she placed me on the spiritual heritage and grand opening committees for the centennial celebration. This was my first experience with city government and officials.

Jeanette understood my heart in most things. We shared a passion to honor God and bless His children in the community, trusted each other, and trusted God's will. The Spiritual Foundation Committee created the Bakersfield Centennial Gospel Night. The event was free to participants and guests and featured church choirs of Bakersfield who ministered through music. Each year for eight consecutive years, the event's attendance grew. It grew so large, in fact, that we had to rent the civic center, and it still holds the record for the largest attendance at a non-ticketed event.

I was at Bakersfield Centennial Gospel Night when Jeanette introduced me to David Voss, the CEO of Jesus Shack of Bakersfield. The vision of this Christian organization is "raising a generation to reach this generation," and it focuses on Christian concerts, street teams and community events.

When Jeanette took the development director position

at Bakersfield Christian High School, she asked if I would serve on the school board. I gladly accepted. The seven years I served on the executive board for the school prepared me to serve on many other boards in the future.

As development director, Jeanette was responsible for turning a small Christian high school into a multimillion-dollar project, which required acquiring land, running a capital campaign to raise the funds needed, and increasing the number of school board members. God allowed me to use my experience opening food service units to design a multipurpose building for the new campus and help it function effectively, from serving lunches to hosting sporting events.

Eventually, Jeanette moved on and became the executive director of the Kern Arts Council. Through her new role and my position at Price Disposal, we were once again able to collaborate, and we developed the first recycled material arts festival in the state of California. The creation of this festival opened my eyes to the truth that when people trust in the vision and purpose of an event, those people will give to make the event happen.

Because of my friendship with Jeanette, I have been able to serve God and bless His children on both state and national levels.

Cancer brought me another friend I do not believe I would have met if I had stayed healthy. In June of 1993, I began treatment with Dr. Alan Cartmell of Comprehensive Blood and Cancer Center (CBCC). He prayed with me every time we met, and he would initiate the prayer. Dr. Cartmell, regardless of the situation, was always positive, and always provided prayer to encourage me. He was with me during the most difficult times, including the three times I learned the cancer had returned. Dr. Cartmell is the one who said he had to take a deep breath before entering my exam room because of how rapidly I was declining.

Over the past twenty-six years, I have seen Dr.

Cartmell every six months to talk about life, family, and grandchildren. He once wrote me a personal note that said, "Ray, you are God's friend, friend to man, my friend." Dr. Cartmell is my friend and gift from God. I appreciate this friend who has willingly spoken on television—as a physician—about God's miracle in my life.

MY PERSONAL RELATIONSHIP WITH CHRIST

*The thief cometh not, but for to steal, and to kill,
and to destroy: I (Jesus) am come that they might
have life, and that they might have
it more abundantly.*

John 10:10

I am an ordinary man who takes out his own trash and who mowed his own yard today. I thank God for all the experiences in my life. I grew up loving to experience life through volunteering and gaining wisdom and knowledge.

I have experienced God the Father, Jesus, and the Holy Spirit as *"[friends] that sticketh closer than [brothers]" (Proverbs 18:24). Whether through navigating the politics of life, providing for my family, fighting for my life because of cancer, or trying to remain focused on God's will during times of success,* God's wisdom and strength have enabled me to do more for God, my family, my career, and my community. He has enabled me to live out my

Marine Corps motto ("Semper Fidelis"/always faithful) and code of conduct (God, Country, Corps/community).

God will use ordinary people who are willing. I was not Pastor Benny Hinn's first or second choice, but I was the one who was willing to respond to God's call. This resulted in my position with Price Family / Price Disposal, and God has created a life for me now that fulfills all that I desire to do for my family, career, and community. God has used this part of my testimony of God's healing a number of times.

I honestly believe in the inspired words of President John F. Kennedy, "Ask not what this country can do for you, but ask what you can do for this country." I also appreciate President Ronald Reagan's famous phrase "peace through strength." To me, this means that if we are strong through faith, we have the ability to live peacefully with God and do His will.

While interviewing me after seeing the Trinity Broadcasting Special *God's Healing Touch*, a reporter commented with enthusiasm, "You must be a great cheerleader for the Lord since your healing." I explained that God had strengthened and deepened my faith to live for Him and my family.

Teresa Allen from Benny Hinn Ministries, whom I got to know by serving with the ministry, once said, "Ray you are the type of standard God rests upon." This was a humbling statement coming from a person I highly respected.

GOD'S WORD

Reading God's Word helped me understand the purpose of the Holy Spirit in my life and how I can help others see Jesus in their lives. This encouraged me. God gives us examples to follow in the Old Testament, and Jesus, in the New Testament, shows us the power of the Holy Spirit in our lives. God the Father, Jesus, and the Holy Spirit are why I do what I do. My favorite books in God's Word are Proverbs, which provides us with God's wisdom, Job, which models how to live through crisis, and James, which shows us how to live a Christian life.

The Bible showed me how men of God lived out their faith without all the things we have today that we take for granted. Praise God that I understood the purpose of the Bible in my life before the cancer. I would not have had the spiritual and mental strength to live through the cancer without God's Word. As a Marine, I knew of the strength of God's mighty warriors of Israel. My surgeon, Mark Newbrough, said the miracle of my healing allows me to stand as an example of my faith.

My favorite verse is Isaiah 40:31 (NIV): "But they that wait upon the Lord shall renew their strength; they shall mount up with wings as eagles; they shall run, and not be weary; and they shall walk, and not faint." I take "wait upon" to mean serve the Lord, being active in one's faith and personal relationship with God. I ask myself continually how I can honor God and bless His children.

I enjoy facilitating the operational needs of a community event, which enables the event leadership to focus on the intentions of the event. This follows the example of Jesus, who came to serve and not be served. When good people do nothing, evil persists, but when godly, beautiful people have strength and constantly move forward, they lift up themselves and others around them.

I keep God's Word fresh daily by watching Christian television channels like Trinity Broadcasting Network, Hillsong channel, and The Word Network. Also, I receive biblical emails from Christian ministries, and I listen to Christian music in my vehicle each morning on my way to work. This allows me to rest in God's grace in my life, which gives me the desire and tools to share God's grace with others.

MY MOST FREQUENT PRAYER

I know that I have made mistakes in all areas of my life. God has given me the ability to examine myself after making a mistake, so I can avoid making the same mistake again. Through my life, I have learned that God does not move away from me, but that I have moved away from God. Sometimes this happens because I think I can do things on my own. Therefore, I often pray "God protect me from myself." This is especially important when it comes to the relationships in my life: marriage, children, family, friends, employers, and employees.

I learned early on that people do not want to be preached to, but rather shown God's love and favor through actions. One of the greatest examples of God protecting me from myself was when he controlled my tongue when I was dealing with Social Security during the cancer. I checked with Social Security every time they sent benefits for me and my family. I made notes of the date, time, and person whom I spoke with for each telephone call and kept a social security file, which is my natural practice as a manager.

In 1996, when we purchased our first house, Social Security was claiming we were overpaid by $16,000 and requested that we pay it back. Even though I sent them all my documentation, it took six months to get a sit-down meeting with a social security manager to discuss our situation. Once the appointment was set, I began praying for wisdom to know how to speak and what to say to the manger I would meet with. Just before entering the building, I asked God to "give me the words to say or shut my mouth." I walked into the office and stated that I had an appointment, and the staff brought me to a conference room and sat me at the table. The manager walked in with a huge four-inch binder, sat down, and began speaking: "Mr. Scott, Social Security recorded everything you wrote and every telephone call you made. In all my years of working with Social Security, I have never seen someone do everything you did to ensure that the information Social Security gave you was correct, and yet everything backfired on you. This amount is too great for me to waive without sending to a panel to review, but I am recommending that it be waived. You will receive the final decision in the mail." I stood up, shook the manager's hand, and said thank you. This meeting was on a Wednesday, and I received Social Security's decision to waive the total amount on that Friday. When have you ever heard of or seen a federal agency resolve an issue and send official documents in two days? That can only be explained by the favor of God.

PRAISE AND WORSHIP

My closeness to God grows stronger through praise and worship. For me, this time with God creates "a peace that surpasses all understanding." During praise and worship, I focus solely on loving God, and God reveals His inspired will for me. God inspired me to use my talents for work issues, church ministry needs, community events, and to help with family and friends. The purpose of the Bakersfield Centennial Gospel Night was to simply create an atmosphere for the Holy Spirit to minister to people through music. God brought Pastor Ron Crenshaw of Shekinah Ministries and his congregation to the Bakersfield Centennial Gospel Night the first year, and they took care of the technical details of the event. This allowed me to focus on the administration of the event, which is my gift or talent. Pastor Ron agreed with God's vision for the event and was willing to serve. Matthew

5:8 (NIV) says "Blessed are the pure in heart, for they will see God." The event existed to honor God and bless His children, which increased my faith and helped me trust God and do His will, because I know that what God inspires, God will provide for.

GOD'S UNCONDITIONAL LOVE

One night during the cancer, my wife and children could not even hold me because I had a long needle sticking out of my chest for chemotherapy, so I was feeling very alone and depressed. Then, the Holy Spirit gave me a vision of God my Father holding me in His arms, close to His chest as His child, and I felt loved, secure, and protected.

For me, faith is the belief in God that enables me to live life, walk through fear, and love myself and others with a love that can only come from God. This love has saved me from myself, including all the errors in my life, and it allows me to show God's love to others. When I have the opportunity, I pray that God's anointing falls on people, as I experienced when I received God's healing from cancer. God's unconditional love for me has brought people into my life to encourage me through life's challenges and be with me during times of success.

In 2011, as Ashley and I were preparing for Deann's birthday party, I had to go to the emergency room once again. The food had just arrived from the caterer,

MY CANCER GOD'S MERCY

balloons and decorations had been set, and I went to see if Ashley was done getting Deann's hair ready for the party. I walked into the bedroom, and they both looked at me and said, "What happened?" Because Ashley and I were focused on making this day special for Deann, we forgot that the balloons were latex, which I am very allergic to. Latex had caused anaphylactic shock because of all of my surgeries.

My face immediately started swelling up, but, praise God, we were living very close to the emergency room. I drove myself to the ER, so Deann and Ashley could take care of the party with family and friends. I walked into the emergency room, and it was so apparent what was happening that they immediately sent me to the procedure room, despite all the other people waiting to be seen. They placed me in the room they use for people brought in by ambulances. In a room with eight beds separated only by curtains, the doctors quickly gave me an epinephrine injection, told me to rest, and let me know that they would be coming in and out frequently to monitor me.

For the first two hours, I was by myself. Then, an ambulance brought in a woman who had been found non-responsive by her family while taking a nap. They cared for her in the bed right next to me, and I could clearly hear everything the paramedics did for her in an attempt to bring her back. Then, I heard a doctor say they needed to pronounce the time of death. After praying for

MY PERSONAL RELATIONSHIP WITH CHRIST

her family's peace, I completely understood the saying, "There, but for the grace of God, go I." Once again, this deepened my faith in God.

MY FINAL THOUGHTS

One of my greatest sources of pride has been my work with an extraordinary organization called Keep California Beautiful. Keep California Beautiful is a non-profit organization dedicated to educating, engaging and encouraging California residents in recycling, beautification, and community networking. It works with diverse groups and organizations across the state to connect local affiliates and form communities. In my service to Keep California Beautiful, I am using what I learned as a Marine in Cairo, Egypt: "No man is too big to pick up another man's foreign object or debris." In 2013, I was asked to consider being the board president for Keep California Beautiful.

God uses ordinary people to do extraordinary things in this world. That explains how God used a man who was destined to die four times in 1994 from the complications of cancer to serve as board president of Keep California Beautiful. All I did was simply honor God and encourage His children.

If you have not asked Jesus Christ to be your Lord and Savior, I pray that this testimony of God the Father, Jesus, and the Holy Spirit in my life encourages you to do so. Amen.

When the Bible says God is not a respecter

of persons, this means He does not ignore or change His standards for anyone. The Bible teaches that God knows our thoughts and, consequently, our hearts. God loves you as He loves me. Amen!

Ask Jesus to be the Lord of your life, receive forgiveness of your sin, believe and confess with your mouth that Jesus is the Lord of your life, and receive the gift of salvation and eternal life. Amen.

1010 Washington Blvd., Stamford, CT 06901
T: 203.659.3000 F: 203.659.3001
info@kab.org / www.kab.org

Keep America Beautiful Recycling Hero Awards 2022
(presented at the annual conference of the Solid Waste Association of North America, December 2022)

Keep American Beautiful Individual Recycling Hero Award

The individual hero award is presented to Sergeant Ray Scott, Retired U.S. Marine Corps who has been a driving force in supporting and promoting recycling across California.

As the past president of Keep California Beautiful, Ray has inspired the next generation of leaders through the development of K-12 and collegiate environmental education and stewardship programs. Overseeing the development of a mobile APP to promote citizen science and prevent litter, Scott's 22-year effort has left a legacy to encourage individuals to act every day to improve their community.

His legacy to educate, engage, and encourage Californians to recycle will be long remembered and built upon. And his legacy of service as a leader and champion of Keep America Beautiful is additionally commended by the board of directors of Keep America Beautiful who in their last meeting noted his commitment and dedication.

Ray, we are grateful for your service.

Jennifer K. Lawson
President and CEO
Keep America Beautiful

APPENDIX

Resources:

Visit https://ordinarymanextraordinarygod.com for supporting documents and videos.

Awards:

Keep America Beautiful Individual Recycling Award

• awarded annually on or around America Recycles Day, to honor an active or retired military member that demonstrate the tremendous potential of the U.S. military to improve recycling across the country

• presented to Ray Scott on December 6, 2022 at the annual conference of the Solid Waste Association of North America

• presented by Jennifer Lawson, President and CEO of Keep America Beautiful

CONTACT INFORMATION

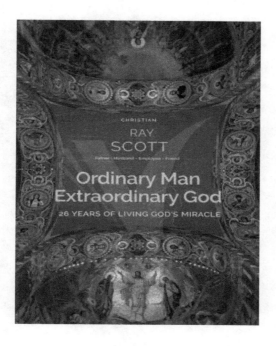

Ray can be reached for prayer requests at
info@ordinarymanextraordinarygod.com.

CPSIA information can be obtained
at www.ICGtesting.com
Printed in the USA
BVHW051921220223
659019BV00011B/107